the
sanctuary
soloist

*A collection of vocal solos
by leading composers
for use in worship service
or concert*

high voice

Compiled and Edited by

fred bock

Also published for Low Voice

If you have enjoyed this collection of fine solos you will certainly enjoy THE SANCTUARY SOLOIST
Volume #2, High Voice—BG0767, Low Voice—BG0768.

fOREWORD

Back in 1964, when THE SANCTUARY SOLOIST first appeared, it was received with open arms by singers around the country. Here was a collection of refreshing and contemporary vocal solos for use either in church, or study, or in concert. The National Association of Teachers of Singing *Bulletin* gave the book a rave review. I was very pleased. I like this book above all the others I have compiled. My initial concept was to set well-known hymns in new garb. It seemed to me that when musicians gathered to complain about the state of music in the church, their complaints were usually directed at the music rather than the text. What this meant to me was that the truths of the texts remained, but because of cultural changes in our world, the music to which they were originally set had lost its impact. The answer was to create new settings. To do this, I called on all my friends who write music. They eagerly responded with the material you hold in your hand. Along the way we altered our Plan "A" to include some non-hymns as well. But with good reason. We all know the problems surrounding Mother's Day. In spite of the efforts of the Hallmark greeting card people, this is not a holy day. However, every church I've been to or served in wants to at least make a token nod of recognition to the mothers of the congregation on this their Special Day. We've all seen that routine of finding the oldest mother, the mother who travelled the farthest, the mother with the most children, and so on. In an effort to provide an alternative to all that, we were thrilled when Paul Sjolund showed us A MOTHER'S LOVE. Here is a text we can all believe, and I know you will find Paul's setting to be sensitive and very usable. The David Raksin piece, PSALM ON THE EVE OF BATTLE and Robert Elmore's SLEEP, HOLY BABE are the other two departures from our original concept. The rest are straight out of the hymnal in the pew.

But here we are in 1980. After several years of THE SANCTUARY SOLOIST being out of print by its original publisher, it is once again available. The book is just like it was with one exception. We have replaced the original setting of JESUS, THE VERY THOUGHT OF THEE with the popular Eric Thiman setting. And what a lovely setting it is. If you've never heard this one, I know you will agree that it fits in nicely with the style of the others and that it is a decided plus to our publication.

Let me tell those of you who are seeing this book for the first time that we have a cassette recording of soprano Marilyn Powell singing all of these selections accompanied by yours truly at the pianoforte. The catalog number of the cassette is B-G7519. By listening to Marilyn's marvelous renditions you will get a good idea of what these songs are all about. Marilyn was soprano soloist for many years at Hollywood Presbyterian Church in Los Angeles, and now is soloist on the "Hour of Power" television show from Garden Grove Community Church. She is a very active recording-studio singer which means that she can sing *anything* in *any style* and *well!* I urge you to get ahold of the cassette. It will help your performance.

Well, that's the story on this book. I am grateful to the original publishers, Word, Inc. for assigning this publication to Fred Bock Music Company so that we might once again make available these fine vocal solos.

Fred Bock
January, 1980

table of contents

" *I wish to see all arts, principally music, in the service of Him who gave and created them. Music is a fair and glorious gift of God. I would not for the world forego my humble share of music. Singers are never sorrowful, but are merry, and smile through their troubles in song. Music makes people kinder, gentler, more staid and reasonable. I am strongly persuaded that after theology there is no art that can be placed on a level with music; for besides theology, music is the only art capable of affording peace and joy of the heart ... the devil flees before the sound of music almost as much as before the Word of God.* "

— MARTIN LUTHER

A Mother's Love

GRACE NOLL CROWELL*

PAUL T. SJOLUND
(A.S.C.A.P.)

*Used by permission of the author

God's own voice speak-ing thru her lips, The words that will bear

fruit-age for e - ter - ni - ty.

And I can feel him in a moth-er's touch; A - cross the wid-'ning years, Her

shield-ing hands will still reach out as if to keep from harm her lit-tle child,—How

well God un-der-stands a moth-ers heart, So like His own it is!

True moth - er-hood has touched His gar-ments hem for strength and

wis-dom, And, sure - ly, O God, we hon-or Thee the day we

hon - or them.

Draw Thou My Soul

Words by
LUCY LARCOM

Music by
JANET SANBORN

Lead forth my soul__ O__ Christ one with Thine own

Joy-ful to fol - low__ Thee__ thru paths un-known.

In Thee my faith re - new__ Give me Thy work to do

Thru me Thy truth be shown Thy love made known.

Not for my-self_ a - lone_ may my prayer be;

Lift Thou my soul_ O_ Christ clo - ser to Thee:

Cleanse it from guilt and wrong, Teach it sal - va - tion's song:

Till earth and heav'n ful-fill God's ho-ly will._

How Sweet The Name Of Jesus Sounds

Lyrics by
JOHN NEWTON

Music by
FRED BOCK (A.S.C.A.P.)

12

Jesus, The Very Thought of Thee

Ascribed to St. Bernard
of Clairvaux, 1091-1153
Tr. Edward Caswall, 1814-78

Music by
Eric H. Thiman.

Nor voice can sing, nor heart can frame, Nor can the

mem - 'ry___ find A sweet-er sound than

Thy blest name, O Sa-viour of man - kind.

O Hope___ of ev - 'ry

con - trite heart, O Joy___ of___ all___ the meek,___ To those who

fall how kind___ Thou art, How good___ to those who

seek! But what___ to___ those who find? ah,___

this Nor tongue___ nor pen___ can show;___ The love of

Je - - sus,____ what it is____ None but His loved ones

know.

Je-su, our

Jesus, Thou Joy Of Loving Hearts

Words Anonymous
Translated by Ray Palmer (1858)

Music by
LYN MURRAY (A.S.C.A.P.)

More Love to Thee, O Christ

Words by
Elizabeth Prentiss

Music by
RALPH CARMICHAEL
(A.S.C.A.P.)

More love to Thee, more love to Thee. Once earth-ly joy I craved, sought peace and rest. Now Thee a - lone I seek, give what is best. This all my pray'r shall be: More love O Christ to Thee more love to Thee, more love to Thee,

Then shalt my lat - est breath _____ whis - per Thy

praise _____ This be the part-ing cry. _____

My heart shall raise This still its pray'r shall be: More love, O

Christ, to Thee, more love to Thee, more love to Thee. _____

add Pedal

Manuals

add Pedal

no breath

ritard.

Optional

O Love That Wilt Not Let Me Go

Words by
GEORGE MATHESON

Music by
RICHARD ELLSASSER
(A.S.C.A.P.)

yield my flick'ring torch to Thee; My heart re-stores its bor-rowed ray,

That in thy sun-shine's blaze its day May bright-er, bright-er, fair-er

be.

O joy that seek-est me through pain, I

* for piano performance, left hand should play bass clef notes one octave higher, and down stem notes in treble clef.

can-not close my heart to thee;   I   trace the rain-bow through the rain,   And

feel   the pro-mise   is   not   in vain That morn shall tear - less   be,

poco a poco cresc.

tear - less   be.

f molto rit.

Molto maestoso

ff

O Cross,   O Cross

Organ (Solo stop)

ff

molto rit.

p   *molto*

meno mosso

* for piano performance, raise bass notes one octave when necessary.

O Cross that lift-est up my head, I dare not ask to fly from Thee; I lay in dust life's glo-ry dead, And from the ground there blos-soms red Life, Life, that shall end-less be. O Love that will not let me go.

* May be performed one octave lower if unable to sing *pp* at this range.

O Master, Let Me Walk With Thee

Words by
WASHINGTON GLADDEN
(1879)

Music by
PAUL SJOLUND
(A.S.C.A.P.)

1. O Mas-ter, let me walk with Thee,_ In low-ly paths of ser-vice free; Tell me Thy se-cret; help me bear The strain of toil, the fret_ of care.
2. Help me the slow of heart to move_ By some_ clear, win-ning word_ of love; Teach me the way-ward feet to stay, And guide them in the home-ward way.

3. Teach me Thy pa - tience; still with Thee,

In clos-er, dear - er com-pa - ny, In work that keeps faith

sweet_ and_ strong, In trust that tri-umphs o - ver wrong.

4. In hope that sends a shin - ing ray Far down ___ the fu - ture's broad - 'ning way; In peace that on - ly Thou canst give, With Thee, ___ O Mas - ter, let ___ me live. ___

Psalm on the Eve of Battle

Words from
The Scriptures

Music by
DAVID RAKSIN (A.S.C.A.P.)

How ma-ny are my foes ___ O Lord! ___ Ma-ny

are they that rise up a-gainst me, Ma-ny are they that say of my soul:

"There is no hope for him in God." But Thou, O Lord, ___

art a shield a-bout me; My glo-ry, and the One who

lift-eth up my head._____ With my

voice I call un-to the Lord ___ and He an-swer-eth me ___

_ out of His Ho - ly moun-tain._____

Spirit Of God

Words by
GEORGE CROLY

Music by
DONALD HUSTAD
(A.S.C.A.P.)

Moderately, with great freedom

Spir - it of God, de-scend up - on my heart;

Wean it from sin, through all its pul-ses move; Stoop to my

weak-ness, might-y as Thou art, And make me love Thee,

love Thee as I ought to love.

rit.

★ On the piano, open chords will be broken

Teach me to feel that Thou art al-ways nigh;

Teach me the strug-gles of the soul to bear, To check the

ris-ing doubt, the reb-el sigh; Teach me the

pa - tience of un-an-swered prayer.

'Tis So Sweet To Trust In Jesus

Words by
LOUISA STEAD

Music by
FRED BOCK (A.S.C.A.P.)

In an easy tempo

1.'Tis so sweet to trust in Je - sus, just to take Him at His
sweet to trust in Je - sus, Pre-cious Je - sus, Sav-ior,

Word; Just to rest up - on His prom - ise; Just to know "Thus saith the
Friend. And I know that Thou art with me, Wilt be

Lord."   2. O how

with me to the end. Je-sus, Je - sus, how I trust Him! How I've

proved Him o'er and o'er! *no hold* Je-sus, Je - sus, pre-cious Je - sus! O for

no breath grace to trust ____ Him more! *A little slower mf ten.* Je-sus, Je - sus, pre-cious

no breath Je - sus! O for grace to trust ____ Him more!

What A Friend We Have In Jesus

Words by
JOSEPH SCRIVEN

Music by
JANET SANBORN

Freely

What a friend we have in Je-sus, All our sins and griefs to bear; What a pri-vi-lege to car-ry Ev-ery-thing to God in prayer; O what peace we of-ten for-feit O what need-less pain we bear: All be-cause we do not car-ry: Ev-ery-thing to God in prayer.

A little faster

Are we weak and heav-y la-den, Cum-bered with a load of care? Pre-cious Sa-vior, still our re-fuge

Take it to the Lord in prayer. Do thy friends de-spise, for-sake thee Take it to the Lord in

prayer In His arms He'll take and shield thee Thou wilt find a so-lace there.

When I survey the wondrous Cross

Words by
Isaac Watts

Music by
LYN MURRAY (A.S.C.A.P.)

Did e'er such love and sor-row meet? or thorns com-pose so rich a crown? Were the whole realm of na-ture mine, that were an off-'ring far too small. Love so a-maz-ing, so di - vine,_____ De-mands my soul, my life, My all!_____

Sleep, Holy Babe

Words by
Rev. E. CASWALL

Music by
ROBERT ELMORE
(A.S.C.A.P.)

How sweet Thy rest, How sweet Thy rest. _____ Sleep Ho - ly Babe Thine An - gels watch a - round, all bend-ing low with fold ed wings be-fore th' in - car - nate King of

Lyrics within the music:

kings,

Be - fore th'in - car - nate King of kings

In rev'rent awe pro - found.

Sleep, Ho-ly Babe. Sleep, Ho-ly Babe.

★Organ: sustain light 16' pedal